# HORSE
# &PONY
# CARE

# HORSE & PONY CARE

Carolyn Henderson

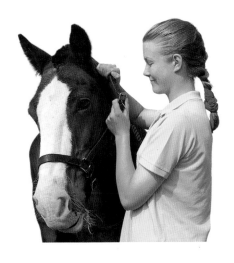

FIREFLY BOOKS

# A DORLING KINDERSLEY BOOK
www.dk.com

Published by Firefly Books Ltd., 2000

First Printing

**Canadian Cataloguing in Publication data**

Henderson, Carolyn
Horse & pony care
(Firefly riding club)
Includes index.
ISBN 1-55209-513-4

1. Horses – Juvenile literature. 2. Ponies – Juvenile literature. I. Title.
II. Title: Horse and pony care. III. Series: Henderson, Carolyn. Firefly riding club.

SF302.H46 2000　　　　　　j636.1　　　　　　C99-931544-7

First Published in Canada in 2000 by
Firefly Books Ltd.
3680 Victoria Park Avenue
Willowdale, Ontario M2H 3K1

**Project Editor** Claire Bampton
**Project Art Editor** Lesley Betts

**For Dorling Kindersley**
**Series Editor** Maggie Crowley　**Series Art Editor** Sharon Grant
**Editor** Kathleen Bada　**Designer** Darren Holt
**DTP Designer** Nomazwe Madonko
**Photographers** Andy Crawford and John Henderson
**Production** Lisa Moss
**Picture Researcher** Francis Vargo
**Jacket design** Margherita Gianni

**Managing Editor** Jayne Parsons
**Managing Art Editor** Gill Shaw

Colour reproduction by Colourscan, Singapore
Printed and bound in Italy by L.E.G.O.

# CONTENTS

# FOREWORD

CARING FOR A HORSE OR PONY takes a lot of time and work, but is great fun. This book shows you all you need to know – how to catch, feed, and groom a pony and how to keep it happy, healthy, and safe in the stable and in the pasture. Even if you don't have a pony of your own, spending time looking after it means you get to know how it behaves and reacts. Caring for a pony is a big responsibility, but this book will help you enjoy it!

# CONFORMATION, COLORS, AND MARKINGS

To describe or assess a horse, look at its conformation, coat color, and any markings. Good conformation, or shape, means that the horse has correct proportions. Different breeds and types have different characteristics, but the guidelines for good conformation are always the same.

## Points of a Horse

The points of the horse are names given to parts of its head, body, and legs. They are like reference points on a map. Some parts have unusual names, such as the withers, so many people find it useful to learn all the points of a horse.

Crest

Poll

Ears

Forelock

Mane

Throat

Chin groove

Mouth

Jugular groove

Windpipe

Dock

Croup

Loins

Back

Shoulder

Withers

**Shoulders** that are powerful and sloping are found in more athletic horses. This feature makes them more comfortable to ride.

Chest

Stifle

Flank

Ribs

Belly

Thigh

Elbow

Forearm

Gaskin

Chestnut

Knee

Hock

Fetlock joint

Cannon bone

Pastern

Heel

Ergot

Coronet

Wall of hoof

**Hooves** are shock absorbers so they must be well cared for.

## CONFORMATION

**A HORSE'S CONFORMATION**
Good conformation means more than good looks. It allows a horse to stand up to hard work because there is less strain on its body and legs. Judging conformation takes practice, but in general a horse's body should look symmetrical. Although all horses have strong and weak points, ideally the strong points compensate for the weak ones.

*Back must be strong to carry rider.*

*Both pairs of legs should be straight with the hooves pointing forward.*

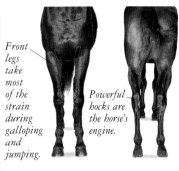

*Front legs take most of the strain during galloping and jumping.*

*Powerful hocks are the horse's engine.*

## BASIC COLORS

**BASIC COAT COLORS**
Coat colors are either solid or spotted. Color is often used to describe a horse. It does not affect a horse's performance, but many people have preferences. Some breeds, such as the Cleveland Bay and Palomino, are almost always the same color – Clevelands are bay and Palominos are gold. Appaloosas have spotted coats in varied patterns, such as blanket and snowflake. Gray horses vary from white to dark gray and can be plain, dappled, or "flea-bitten."

CHESTNUT     GRAY     BAY

DUN     PALOMINO     PAINT

## FACE MARKINGS

**FACE MARKINGS**
Natural patterns of white hair on a horse's face range from those covering the forehead and front of the face to small snips around the mouth. Some horses have more than one face marking, such as a star and snip.

STRIPE     STAR     BLAZE     SNIP

## LEG MARKINGS

**LEG MARKINGS**
Leg markings are usually white. If they come to below the knee or hock they are called socks. If they extend further up the leg they are known as stockings. Black spots on white hair around the coronet are called ermine markings. Hooves can be black, white, or black with white stripes.

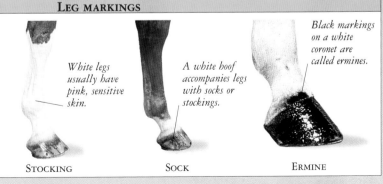

*White legs usually have pink, sensitive skin.*

*A white hoof accompanies legs with socks or stockings.*

*Black markings on a white coronet are called ermines.*

STOCKING     SOCK     ERMINE

# CARING FOR A HORSE OR PONY

LOOKING AFTER A HORSE OR PONY is a big responsibility. A pony needs someone to provide food, shelter, and water, and to keep it fit and healthy. As you spend time cleaning out the stable and grooming a pony, you will learn more about its habits and body language and will be able to assess how it is feeling. Taking care of a pony involves hard work throughout the year, but building a relationship with a pony can be very rewarding.

CHOOSE A PONY CAREFULLY
Try to spend time with different horses and ponies. This will help you avoid making mistakes when deciding which type would suit you best.

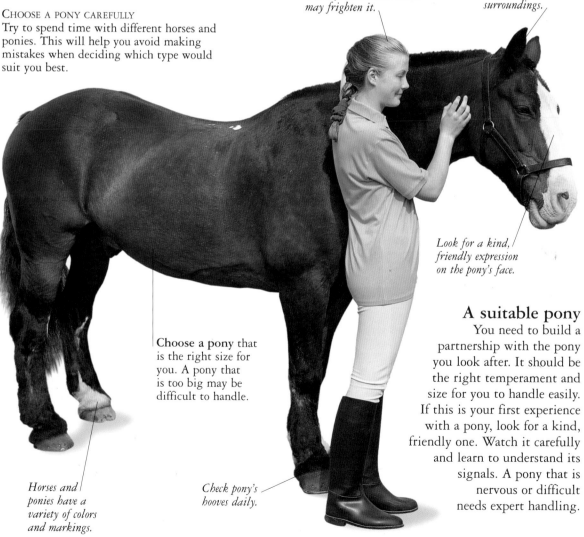

*Treat a pony gently as if it is a friend. Loud noises may frighten it.*

*Ears pointing forward show that the pony is interested and happy with its surroundings.*

*Look for a kind, friendly expression on the pony's face.*

*Choose a pony that is the right size for you. A pony that is too big may be difficult to handle.*

*Horses and ponies have a variety of colors and markings.*

*Check pony's hooves daily.*

## A suitable pony
You need to build a partnership with the pony you look after. It should be the right temperament and size for you to handle easily. If this is your first experience with a pony, look for a kind, friendly one. Watch it carefully and learn to understand its signals. A pony that is nervous or difficult needs expert handling.

*Many young riders start by helping out at a riding school.*

## Helping out

One of the best ways of learning how to look after a pony is to help at a local riding stable. You can learn how to clean stalls, and groom and handle different types of horses and ponies, with experienced people to help you. Spending time at a riding school will help you decide whether you enjoy the commitment before you own or share a pony.

## Grooming kit

Every horse or pony should have its own grooming kit. Wash the brushes regularly and rinse them thoroughly to keep them clean. Do not use one pony's brushes on another, or you might spread skin infections. A pasture-kept pony does not need much grooming as it needs to retain grease in its coat to protect it from the cold and rain. A stabled pony should be groomed more thoroughly.

## Cleaning out

Stables should be cleaned out every day. A four-pronged fork is useful for lifting dirty straw bedding. For cleaning out a shavings bed, use a shavings fork. This allows clean bits of shavings to fall through the gaps, while catching any wet material and droppings. Some tools for cleaning out can also be used to remove droppings from fields. Remember to put your tools away when you have finished with them.

*Hoof dressing*

*Body brush*

*Metal curry comb*

*Plastic curry comb*

*Mane and tail combs*

*Sweat scraper*

*Sponges for the eyes, mouth, and nose, and another for the dock*

*Hoof pick*

*Yard broom*

*Cloth*

*Dandy brush*

*Shovel for picking up small bits of dirty bedding*

*Rubber curry comb*

*Wheelbarrow for collecting manure*

*Waterproof boots*

*Straw fork*

*Shavings fork*

*Rake for raking gravel yard*

*Pitchfork, sometimes used for putting down straw bed*

*Small rake and skip for picking up manure*

# HANDLING A HORSE

HORSES AND PONIES respond best to quiet, confident handling. Keep movements smooth, and be gentle but positive when you touch a horse. Horses are bothered by sudden movements and loud noises; use your voice in a soothing tone to calm and speak sharply, but not loudly, to reprimand.

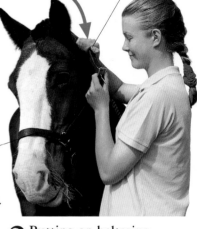

*Be careful not to flip the halter over the horse's head and startle it.*

## Catching a horse

Take your time when trying to catch a horse. Even if you are in a hurry, try to give the impression that you have plenty of time. It is a good idea to occasionally catch a horse, reward it, then let it go, so it does not always associate being caught with being ridden.

*The halter should be fastened securely but not too tightly.*

**2 Putting on haltering**
Slip the lead rope round the horse's neck and put the halter over its nose. Pass the strap behind its ears and fasten.

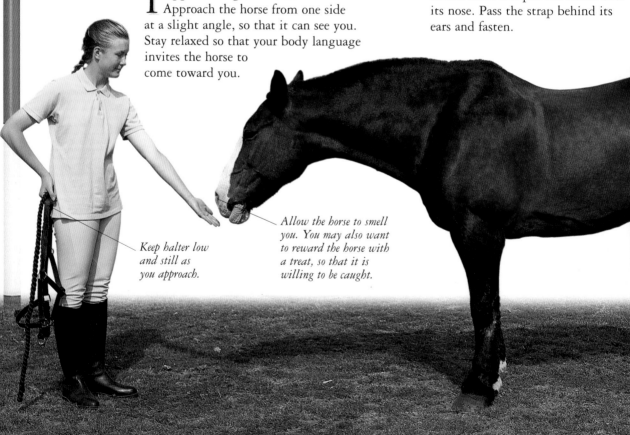

**1 Approaching the horse**
Approach the horse from one side at a slight angle, so that it can see you. Stay relaxed so that your body language invites the horse to come toward you.

*Keep halter low and still as you approach.*

*Allow the horse to smell you. You may also want to reward the horse with a treat, so that it is willing to be caught.*

## Turning a horse out

Open the gate wide enough for easy access and shut it before you let the horse go. Before releasing the horse, turn its head toward the gate, so that you do not get kicked by its hind legs if it gallops off.

## Body language

Watch horses in the field to study their body language. Ears pointing back warn others to stay away. Groups of horses determine their own positions of authority, from the leaders to followers.

*Flattened ears show tension.*

## How to tie a quick-release knot

When tying up a horse, tie the lead rope to a string loop so that if the horse panics the string will break. A quick-release knot is also used to tie up haynets.

**1 Start of knot**
Loop rope through ring. Bring the loose end around and across so that you have made a slanting figure eight.

*This end of the rope attaches to the halter.*

**2 Making the knot**
Pass the loose end behind both thicknesses of rope and then back through the bottom loop of your figure eight.

*Keep loops big so that the rope passes through easily.*

**3 Secure the knot**
Push the loose end back through the loop to make another one. Pull down on the loop you have just made to tighten the knot.

*This is a secure but safe quick-release knot.*

**4 To undo the knot**
To undo the knot, pull on the loose end of the rope. This knot allows you to release a panicking horse quickly and safely.

*Pull on loose end.*

Tying up a horse
When tying up a horse, allow enough length of rope for it to move its head. Some may pull back if they are tied up too short.

*Tie lead rope to piece of string for safety.*

# OUT IN THE FIELD

ALL HORSES AND PONIES should be turned out daily to graze and relax. Some can live out permanently, while others need stabling part of the time. Ponies that have had laminitis should not be turned out on rich spring grass or they may get it again. Horses need fields with safe fencing and gates, clean water, shelter and other horses for company. A field must be large enough to supply all the horses within it enough grass on which to graze and space to roam.

FENCES AND GATES
Gates should be properly balanced and easy to open and close when leading horses through. There are many safe types of fencing, such as post and rail. Never use barbed wire or your horse may injure itself. Check fencing for breaks every day.

## The ideal field

An individual horse needs at least 1 acre (2 hectares) of land on which to graze. Try to graze your horse on grass that has been grown especially for horses – cattle pasture may be too rich. Shelter to protect a horse from wind and rain, and to shade it in summer, can be provided by trees and hedges, or a field shelter. Get expert advice on pasture management, such as fertilizing and resting land.

## Poisonous plants

Check the pasture regularly for poisonous plants. Ragwort is particularly dangerous. It has yellow flowers and should be pulled up and burned immediately – this will help to stop them growing again. Yew, acorns, and deadly nightshade are also dangerous when eaten. Call your vet if you suspect a horse has been poisoned.

*Acorn attached to oak leaf.*

*Yew leaves*

**Post and rail** fencing is safe and strong. Replace broken or weak rails immediately.

*If possible use a pasture where someone can keep an eye on the horses.*

*Grass should be weed free.*

## FRESH WATER

There must always be plenty of clean, fresh water. Use a special water trough or a safe container with no sharp edges. Keep the trough clean and free from things that could contaminate the water, and from ice in winter.

*Horses will go thirsty rather than drink dirty or contaminated water.*

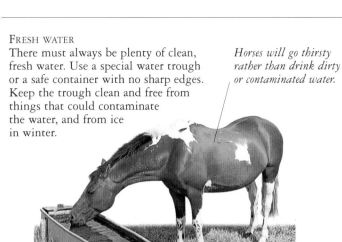

*Water trough should not have sharp edges since these could injure horse.*

## PASTURE MANAGEMENT

• Field must have safe fencing

• There must be a permanent supply of clean, fresh water

• Remove manure from field as often as possible

• Do not turn out ponies susceptible to laminitis on rich grass

• In winter, give hay in the field and, if necessary, extra feed

**Field shelters** must have openings large enough to allow more than one horse to go through at a time. If your field slopes, put your shelter on the highest point so rain drains away from the site.

*Fresh drinking water is supplied in a trough.*

**Trees** and thick hedging provide year-round protection.

*Lighting to help see on dark winter nights.*

# CARE OF A PONY AT PASTURE

**PONIES LIVING OUTDOORS** in a field need daily care and attention. They have special needs at different times of year. For example, they need protection from insects in summer and from cold weather in winter. Check a pasture pony for injury or illness, and make sure that shelter and clean water are always available and the fencing is safe.

### Security measures

Freeze marking is a security system that can help trace a stolen pony. The mark is frozen onto the pony's skin but does not hurt. Each freeze mark is unique. Other systems of identification are hoof branding, identichipping, and lip tattooing.

*Horse is identified by the number.*

### Checking the pony

Go and look over the pony at least once every day. A healthy pony is alert and not shivering. Make sure there are no signs of injury or illness and that its shoes and feet are in good condition. Look out for cuts and any signs of heat or swelling – small cuts may be hidden by a thick coat. Some ponies have pink skin around their noses that may get sunburned in the summer, so use some protective cream.

**Leather halters** or ones with a breakable safety insert should be used. If these get caught up, they are pulled off without injuring the pony.

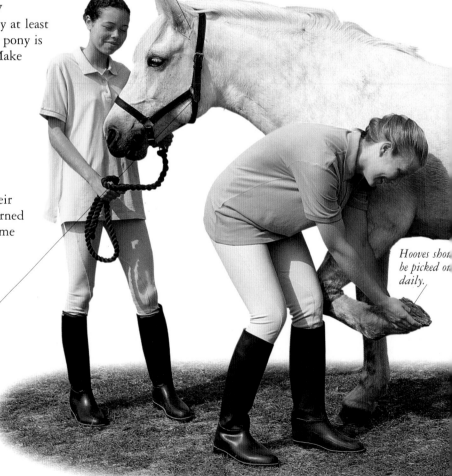

*Base of ears should be warm.*

*Hooves sho[uld] be picked o[ut] daily.*

## Seasonal needs

A pony that lives outdoors needs different kinds of protection at different times of year. It is important that shelter is available all year round to give shade in the summer and protection from wind and rain in the winter.

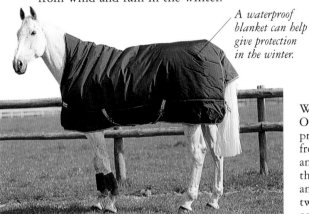

*A waterproof blanket can help give protection in the winter.*

SUMMER NEEDS
Insects are the biggest problem in the summer. Some bite and can cause allergic reactions. Insect repellent helps to control them. You can also use a fly fringe, fastened to a halter, which helps to keep insects away from the pony's eyes.

WINTER NEEDS
Outdoor blankets protect the pony from cold, wind, and rain. Check that they fit correctly and don't rub. Have two blankets in case one gets torn.

*Fly fringe protects pony's eyes from flies.*

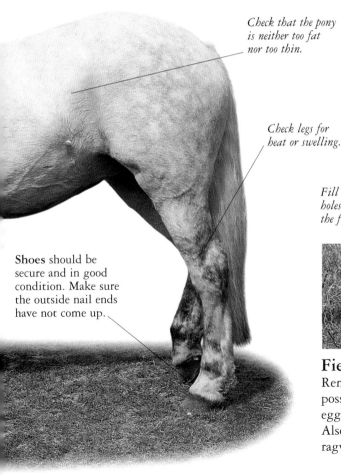

*Check that the pony is neither too fat nor too thin.*

*Check legs for heat or swelling.*

**Shoes** should be secure and in good condition. Make sure the outside nail ends have not come up.

*Removing manure regularly from the field is essential to protect a pony's health.*

*Fill in any holes in the field.*

*Fork through muck you can't pick up.*

## Field care

Remove manure from the field as often as possible. This helps reduce the amount of worm eggs on the field and protect the pony's health. Also, pull up any poisonous plants, such as ragwort, and take them away to be destroyed.

# THE STABLE

THE IDEAL STABLE is designed so that the horses are healthy, happy, and safe and so that the design is convenient for people using the stable. There may be outdoor stables or stables inside a large building called an indoor barn. Feed, hay, and bedding should be stored near the stables, but not so close as to be a fire risk. The stable must be built with safety and security precautions.

**INDOOR BARN**
Indoor barns allow you to clean out and groom out of bad weather. They must have wide central walkways for tying up and leading out horses, and good ventilation and drainage. There should be large doors at each end, which should be left open when possible. Fire precautions are vital inside barns.

## Stall design

Stalls must be light and large enough for a horse to walk around comfortably. Mares with foals need extra large stalls. Good ventilation and drainage are important for a horse's health. Ideally there will be windows at the front and back and ventilation at roof height. Pitched roofs provide more air space, and are therefore preferable to flat roofs.

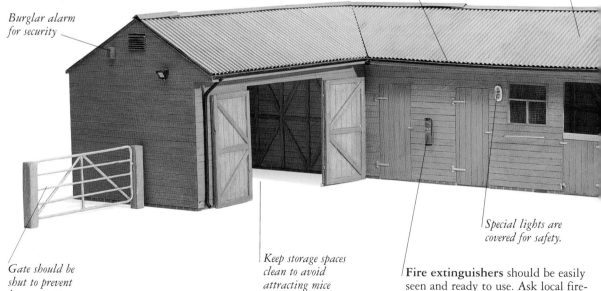

*Pitched roof gives more room for air to circulate.*

*Gutter must be kept clear of falling leaves and other blockages.*

*Burglar alarm for security*

*Gate should be shut to prevent horses escaping from stable.*

*Keep storage spaces clean to avoid attracting mice and rats.*

*Special lights are covered for safety.*

**Fire extinguishers** should be easily seen and ready to use. Ask local fire-fighters for fire prevention advice.

## Bedding materials

Wheat straw is a popular choice for bedding, but it contains a small amount of dust, which makes some horses cough. Paper, wood shavings, hemp, and rubber mats are alternative choices.

SHAVINGS          NEWSPAPER

RUBBER MAT        STRAW

## Cleaning out

Cleaning a stable must be done every day. Clean out completely if you use straw. Shavings, paper, and hemp are more absorbent, so remove manure daily and do a full clean out once or twice a week. If you can, take the horse out of the stable before you begin.

*Dirty bedding is heavy, so only lift a little at a time.*

**1 Remove dirty straw**
To clean out a straw bed, use a four-pronged fork to remove manure and wet, dirty straw. Separate out the clean bedding, then shovel up the dirty bedding into a wheelbarrow.

**2 Brushing up**
Sift through the remaining straw with your fork to check that it is clean. Pile it up round the sides and brush the floor thoroughly. Try to sprinkle some disinfectant on the bare floor once a week.

*Add fresh bedding, piling it higher around the edges.*

**Roof vents** help keep air clean and healthy.

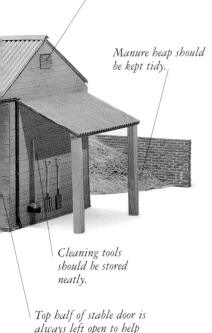

*Manure heap should be kept tidy.*

*Cleaning tools should be stored neatly.*

*Top half of stable door is always left open to help air it out.*

**3 Laying down a bed**
Fork piled up straw into the center of the floor and check that the sides of the stable are clean. Pile fresh straw high around the sides of the stable wall to give added protection to the horse.

# THE STABLED PONY

KEEPING A HORSE or pony in a stable allows you to control what it eats and enables you to keep it clean and healthy. However, looking after a stabled horse or pony takes a lot of time and work and requires you to follow a strict routine. All stabled horses and ponies should be turned out for at least part of the day to keep them happy and relaxed.

*Use your voice firmly but quietly. Some ponies will respond to your voice commands alone.*

## Stable manners

Ponies must be taught to behave well so they are safe to handle in the confined space of a stable. Teach them to step back or move away from you when you apply gentle pressure and use voice commands.

*Anti-weave grid helps to stop pony from weaving over the door.*

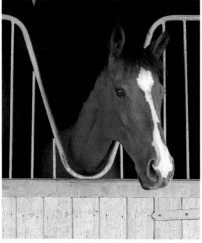

*Hand pressure and voice commands tell the pony to step back. Apply the pressure as short nudges.*

*Boots, especially ones with protective toe caps, are safer than shoes or sandals.*

### STABLE VICES

Ponies who do not like being confined may develop behavioral problems, or stable vices. These include swaying their heads from side to side, called weaving, or biting the stable door, called crib-biting. Ponies with stable vices may be happier when turned out to pasture.

### SAFE CONTROL

Your pony should be happy to obey your commands in the stable. It is important to allow your pony some times of peace and quiet, such as during feed times.

# DAILY ROUTINE

Ponies need a routine to remain healthy and happy. This means feeding them at the same time each day and giving them daily exercise. The combined system can be used where a pony is put out to pasture during the day and kept in a stall at night.

| TIME | STABLE KEPT PONY |
|------|------------------|
| 7:00 AM | Check for any signs of illness or injury. Adjust blankets if necessary and give fresh water and first feed. |
| 7:45 AM | Tie up pony outside stall and clean out. Pick out hooves, remove blankets, and brush over. Exercise now or at a time that suits you, allowing one hour after pony has been fed. |
| 9:15 AM | Tack up and ride out or train. Walk for the last 15 minutes of exercise to allow pony to cool down. Brush over or wash if sweaty, then put on outdoor blanket if weather is bad. Check hooves and shoes and turn out. Wash mangers and buckets. |
| 12:00 PM | Bring in and fully groom. Put on stable blankets. Give second feed and hay and check water. *Put hay in hay net and hang in stable.* |
| 2:00 PM | Check water, give more hay if necessary. Remove manure from stall (pick out). |
| 5:00 PM | Pick out and check water. Add or change blankets if necessary; remember temperature may drop at night. Give third feed and hay. |
| 7:00 – 10:00 PM | Pick out and check water and blankets. Give fourth feed, if required, and more hay. *The stable must be clean for the night.* |

| TIME | COMBINED SYSTEM |
|------|-----------------|
| 7:00 AM | Check pony for illness or injury. Feed and leave to eat in peace. When finished, pick out hooves, put on outdoor blanket if not riding, and turn out. Check water supply and fencing, and give hay in field if necessary. Clean out. |
| 8:00 AM | Brush over and exercise. If pony has been turned out, allow half an hour after bringing in. Make sure pony is cool on return from exercise, brush over or wash down, and check hooves. Fit blanket if necessary and turn out. *Make sure the blanket is fitted securely.* |
| 4:00 PM | Bring in pony and check for signs of injury. Pick out hooves and check shoes. Brush over, change blankets if necessary, and give hay. If wet, use breathable blanket that will transfer moisture away from body. Check one hour later and again if necessary. Change blankets so pony is dry and comfortable for the night. |
| 5:00 PM | Check that pony is dry and warm enough. Give second feed and check water. |
| 7:00 – 9:00 PM | Make sure pony is comfortable. Pick out and check water. Give hay and third feed if necessary. |

# FOOD AND FEEDING

HORSES NATURALLY EAT GRASS and hay, which is called forage. Forage must be of good quality since it is the main part of a horse's diet. When horses have a lot of exercise, they may need extra feed such as a grain mix or other supplement. Small, frequent meals are better for a horse's digestive system than large ones. Make sure clean water is always available. Allow one hour after feeding before you ride.

*Feed your horse small amounts often.*

## The right amount

A horse needs between 1.5 and 2.5 percent of its bodyweight in food each day. For example a 660 lbs (300 kg) pony would need about 16.5 lbs (7.5 kg) food every day. Forage (grass and hay) should provide at least half, and usually more, of the total amount. If a horse is being worked hard, you may need to increase its feed in line with its work. Ask an expert if you are unsure of how much to feed.

*Horses can eat from a bucket or manger.*

## Feeding hay

Hay can be fed on the ground, in a haynet, or in a rack. Soaking hay in clean water helps prevent coughing. If soaking hay, submerge for up to one hour. Never feed a horse dusty or moldy hay.

### 1 Filling haynet
To fill a haynet, hold the top open with one hand and put hay in with the other. Be careful the string around the hay bale doesn't get tangled with the hay.

*Shake hay to remove dust.*

*Pull net to correct height.*

### 2 Placing haynet
Pass haynet drawstring through tie ring and pull the net up. This prevents the horse from getting its foot caught in an empty haynet.

# WHAT TO FEED

Feed pellets or a grain mix (compound feeds), or cereals, such as oats. Compound feeds are best since they are specially formulated; don't add cereals, since they will alter the compound formula.

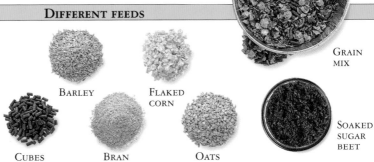

## DIFFERENT FEEDS

### MAIN FOODS
Oats and barley are traditional horse feeds. Flaked corn is fed only in small amounts to horses that are working hard. Bran should not be fed routinely – only feed it as a bran mash on your vet's advice. Sugar beet cubes are a good energy source but must be soaked in water for at least 12 hours before feeding.

BARLEY

FLAKED CORN

GRAIN MIX

SOAKED SUGAR BEET

CUBES

BRAN

OATS

## SUPPLEMENTS

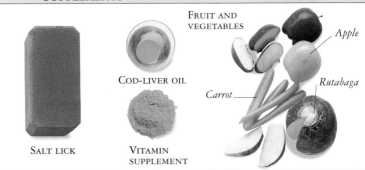

### EXTRAS
All horses should have salt licks available. Horses also enjoy fruit and vegetables, especially carrots and apples, sliced and added to their feed. Some horses may need vitamin and mineral supplements or extras such as cod-liver oil. Always get expert advice before feeding these, since compound feeds already contain the vitamins and minerals a horse needs.

FRUIT AND VEGETABLES

*Apple*

COD-LIVER OIL

*Rutabaga*

*Carrot*

SALT LICK

VITAMIN SUPPLEMENT

## 3 Tying up haynet
Take the end of the drawstring down to the bottom of the haynet and pass it through one of the holes, about two thirds of the way down the haynet. Pull the net up again.

*Pass loose end through the knot so it can't be pulled loose.*

## 4 Fasten knot
Pass the loose end of the drawstring behind the other piece and pull it through in a loop. Pull down with both hands to make a slip knot that is secure but easy to undo.

*Pull up net to tie ring.*

## How to weigh a horse
To calculate a horse's approximate weight use a weigh tape, which measures a horse's girth. This gives corresponding weights to measurements and enables you to decide how much to feed your horse.

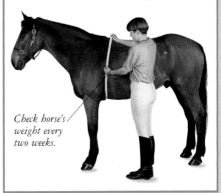

*Check horse's weight every two weeks.*

# GROOMING

DAILY GROOMING helps keep a pony clean and its coat, skin, and hooves healthy. Grooming also helps you get to know a pony and to check for any problems, such as heat in the legs, that may occur. A grooming kit contains special tools that are used for different purposes; keep brushes clean and only use them on the horse they belong to.

*Use hoof pick from heel to toe.*

**PICKING OUT HOOVES**
Use a hoof pick to clean a pony's hooves daily. Work downward, from heel to toe, and do not dig into the V-shaped frog.

*Use the hand nearest the horse's body to groom, since it is easier to to put your weight into the brush strokes.*

*Tie the pony up outside, so that dust from grooming doesn't affect its breathing.*

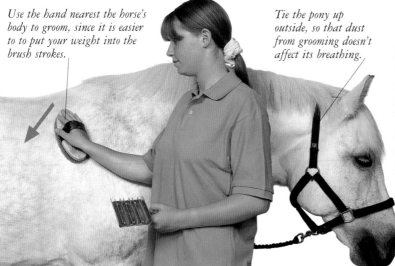

## How to groom
Begin grooming by loosening the dirt in the coat with a rubber currycomb or groomer. Use a dandy brush to flick off loose mud. Using short strokes, remove oil with a body brush. Brush the mane and tail with a body brush or an ordinary hairbrush to avoid breaking the hair. Finally clean the eyes, nose, and dock.

**1 Brushing pony over**
Before riding out, brush your pony over and pick out its feet. Make sure that there is no dirt or dried mud on parts of the pony where tack or blankets will rest, since this might irritate. Check for mud on the back and girth areas, behind the elbows, the face, and the base of the ears.

**USING A CURRYCOMB**
To clean the body brush scrape it against a metal currycomb, then knock out the dust from the currycomb. Never use metal currycombs on a horse.

**2 Cleaning eyes, nose, and dock**
Use separate sponges, or pieces of cotton wool, to clean the eyes, nose, and dock. Dampen the sponges or cotton wool, then gently wipe the necessary parts of the pony. If your pony has a runny nose or weeping eye there may be a problem, so ask an expert for advice.

*Always wash the sponge after use.*

## Care of a pasture-kept pony

Ponies that live outside need the natural oils in their coats to protect them from cold and wet. Before you ride a pasture-kept pony, remove dried mud with a rubber currycomb, then brush over with a dandy or whisk brush. Do not use a body brush on the pony's coat since it takes out the oils; only use a body brush to tidy the mane and tail. Finally pick out the hooves, and clean eyes, nose, and dock.

*Thick coat has natural grease, which protects against wind and rain.*

## Bathing a pony

Only bathe a pony on a warm day. Wet the coat, then work the shampoo into the horse's coat with a sponge or shampoo glove. Rinse thoroughly, then repeat if necessary. Once finished, walk pony around until it is dry.

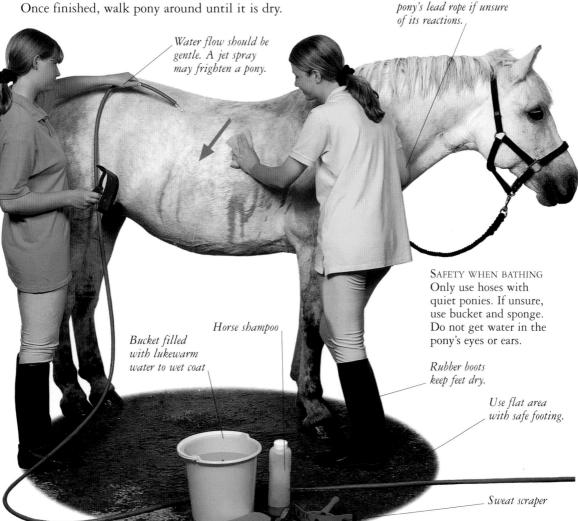

*Water flow should be gentle. A jet spray may frighten a pony.*

*Helper should hold onto pony's lead rope if unsure of its reactions.*

*Bucket filled with lukewarm water to wet coat*

*Horse shampoo*

SAFETY WHEN BATHING
Only use hoses with quiet ponies. If unsure, use bucket and sponge. Do not get water in the pony's eyes or ears.

*Rubber boots keep feet dry.*

*Use flat area with safe footing.*

*Sweat scraper*

# MANES AND TAILS

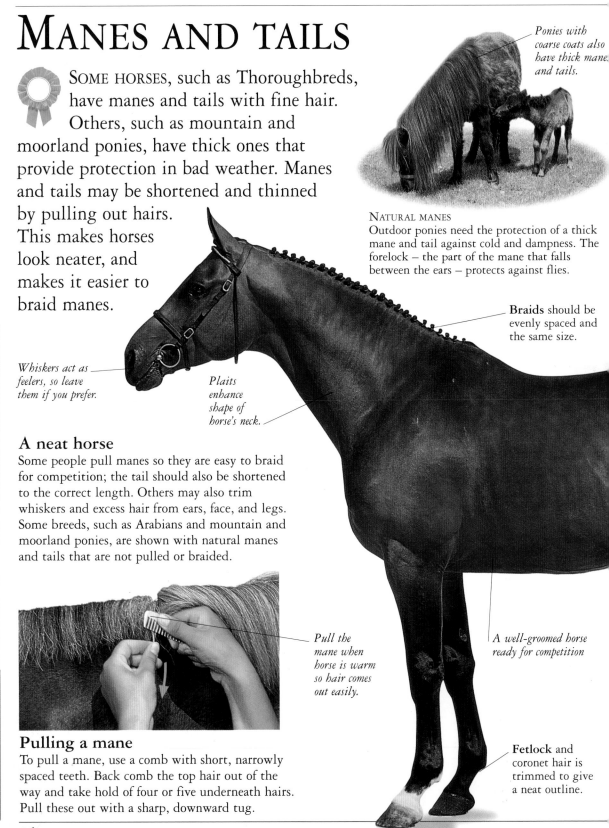

SOME HORSES, such as Thoroughbreds, have manes and tails with fine hair. Others, such as mountain and moorland ponies, have thick ones that provide protection in bad weather. Manes and tails may be shortened and thinned by pulling out hairs. This makes horses look neater, and makes it easier to braid manes.

*Ponies with coarse coats also have thick manes and tails.*

NATURAL MANES
Outdoor ponies need the protection of a thick mane and tail against cold and dampness. The forelock – the part of the mane that falls between the ears – protects against flies.

**Braids** should be evenly spaced and the same size.

*Whiskers act as feelers, so leave them if you prefer.*

*Plaits enhance shape of horse's neck.*

## A neat horse
Some people pull manes so they are easy to braid for competition; the tail should also be shortened to the correct length. Others may also trim whiskers and excess hair from ears, face, and legs. Some breeds, such as Arabians and mountain and moorland ponies, are shown with natural manes and tails that are not pulled or braided.

*Pull the mane when horse is warm so hair comes out easily.*

*A well-groomed horse ready for competition*

## Pulling a mane
To pull a mane, use a comb with short, narrowly spaced teeth. Back comb the top hair out of the way and take hold of four or five underneath hairs. Pull these out with a sharp, downward tug.

**Fetlock** and coronet hair is trimmed to give a neat outline.

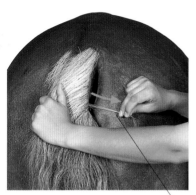

PULLING A TAIL
Tail pulling creates a neat shape but some horses object to it. Stand to the side and pull three or four underneath hairs at a time from each side until you reach halfway down the dock (tail bones). If the horse is unhappy, stop or you may get kicked.

*Pull quickly downwards.*

## Trimming a tail
It takes two people to trim a tail – one to hold out the tail at the angle it is carried when the horse moves, the other to cut. Cut straight across the bottom at the correct length. The top of a full tail – one that has not been pulled – can be braided.

*Avoid pulling front tail hairs – hair will stick up as it grows.*

*Usual length is 4 in (10 cms) below the point of the hock.*

*Tail end should be level when horse is on the move.*

## Putting on a tail bandage
A tail bandage encourages the hair of a pulled tail to lie flat. It also protects the tail hair from being rubbed out when traveling in a trailer.

*Start with bandage rolled so tapes are on the inside.*

### 1 From the top
Start at the top and bandage down to the end of the tail bone. Keep pressure firm and even, but not too tight.

### 2 Tying up
Wrap tapes around, tie in a bow at the front, and tuck in ends. Bend the tail gently into its normal position.

*Tapes should be fastened no tighter than the bandage.*

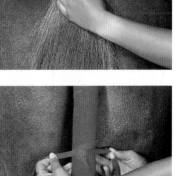

# HOOVES AND SHOEING

A HORSE'S HOOVES, or feet, bear a lot of weight and help cushion the impact when a horse runs or jumps. In the wild, horses' hooves wear down naturally as they roam large distances, however domesticated horses need their hooves trimmed regularly by a farrier. Most working horses need metal shoes to protect their hooves on hard surfaces.

*Rubbery frog absorbs jolts when hoof hits the ground.*

*Bar*

## Parts of the hoof
The hoof is a hard outer shell that encases sensitive structures such as bones, blood vessels, and cartilage. The bottom part is made up of the sole and a V-shaped wedge called the frog.

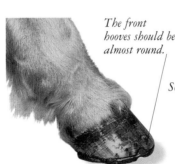

*The front hooves should be almost round.*

*Sole*

*Toe*

*Hard wall*

### FOOT CONFORMATION
Good foot conformation is when the front and hind hooves each form a pair that are the same size and shape.

*Regular trimming keeps the hoof in shape and prevents splits.*

### UNDERSIDE OF THE HOOF
The sole should be slightly concave rather than flat to help the horse grip the ground. The V-shaped frog acts as a pump for the hoof's blood supply.

## How to check a horse's hooves
Check your horse's shoes and pick out its hooves once a day. Unpleasant smells, other than normal stable smells, are a sign of infection.

**2 Get horse to pick up hoof**
Squeeze the fetlock and use your voice to encourage the horse to pick up its hoof.

*Keep your hand on the inside, not the outside of the horse's leg.*

*Make sure the horse is standing square before picking up a hoof.*

**1 Check the leg**
Stand to one side, and run your hand down the leg checking for abnormalities.

**3 Hold the hoof**
As the horse lifts its hoof, catch the toe. Do not lift the leg too high.

*Try not to hold the hoof up for long periods.*

## Dressing the hoof

Cosmetic hoof dressings give a shiny appearance to the hoof. They are used after grooming, for special occasions such as shows. Do not use hoof dressings without asking your farrier's or vet's advice, as some may not be suitable for your horse's feet.

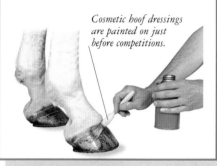

*Cosmetic hoof dressings are painted on just before competitions.*

## Shoeing a horse

Horses are shod to enable them to work in comfort. Sometimes special studs are screwed into the shoes to give extra grip for jumping and galloping.

*Horseshoe nails have flat, square heads.*

*Well-shaped hoof in good condition that has been recently shod*

WHEN TO SHOE
Horses and ponies should have their shoes removed and their hooves trimmed every six weeks. Worn shoes should be replaced.

WELL-SHOD HOOF
The shoe should be shaped to fit the hoof, not the other way around. Nailing the shoes on does not hurt the horse.

## The farrier

A farrier, who makes horseshoes and shoes horses, needs a dry, well-lit area in which to work. Horses can be shod cold or hot. Both methods use nails to keep the shoe in place, however during hot shoeing the shoe is burnt on, which often gives a better fit.

*The farrier will appreciate a quiet, well-mannered horse.*

**Curved knife**, called drawing knife, for trimming hoof

**Protective leather apron** on which farrier can rest horse's leg

**Frog** is sensitive and must not be punctured.

*The horse should be ready when the farrier arrives, and have clean legs and hooves.*

**Hind hooves** are slightly smaller than front hooves.

# CLIPPING

HORSES ARE CLIPPED if their winter coats are too thick for them to work or be ridden without sweating. A horse may need several clips during one season. The type of clip depends on the horse's lifestyle and workload; the more work it does, the less winter coat it should have. A clipped horse needs to wear blankets indoors and out so that it is warm when not working. Some horses are nervous when clipped, and must be handled by experts.

### NATURAL COATS
All horses and ponies grow winter coats. Breeds such as British native ponies have thicker winter coats, as protection against wind and rain, than horses with a lot of Thoroughbred or Arab blood, which are kept in stables.

## Types of clip
There are several different types of clip. Sometimes a lot of hair is removed from horses that work hard. Those that perform lighter work, or that spend most of their time outdoors, need some of their natural coat left on.

### HUNTER CLIP
The hunter clip is used on horses that work hard and fast. All of the coat is clipped except that on the legs and sometimes under the saddle.

*Thick leg hair protects the horse against mud and thorns.*

### BLANKET CLIP
Leaving a blanket-shaped area over the back of the horse unclipped helps keep the horse's back warm. Hair is also left on the legs, but is clipped off the neck. This type of clip allows a hard-working horse to keep cool.

## Clipping a horse

Always clip a horse in a dry, light area, and never outdoors when it is wet or windy. Be careful when using electric clippers – they can be dangerous. Only experts should clip inexperienced or nervous horses.

*Trim the hair from the edges of the horse's ears only, not inside.*

*Keep the folded blanket on the pony so it does not get cold.*

*Clip in smooth sweeps against the direction of the hair growth.*

*Someone holds the horse and gives it confidence while another person clips.*

## Care of a clipped horse

A clipped horse must be kept warm and dry with blankets. If kept indoors, a horse must have a well ventilated, but not drafty, area. Blankets with neck covers and tail flaps give extra protection. A fully-clipped horse may need to wear an exercise sheet when out riding.

*Before putting the blanket on remove loose hair.*

*Head is either clipped fully or clipped up to the bridle cheekpieces, with hair left on the front of the face.*

*Coat is clipped off the underside of the neck, where horses often sweat.*

TRACE CLIP
The trace clip is suitable for hardy horses that live outdoors most of the time. It reduces sweating but leaves some protection. The trace clip gets its name because it was designed for harness horses and follows the lines of the harness traces.

*A trace-clipped horse may need to wear a blanket when resting.*

31

# BLANKETS AND BLANKETING

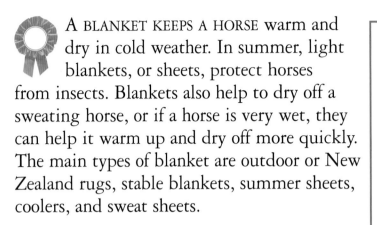

A BLANKET KEEPS A HORSE warm and dry in cold weather. In summer, light blankets, or sheets, protect horses from insects. Blankets also help to dry off a sweating horse, or if a horse is very wet, they can help it warm up and dry off more quickly. The main types of blanket are outdoor or New Zealand rugs, stable blankets, summer sheets, coolers, and sweat sheets.

## Measuring up

A blanket must be the correct size to stay in place. Measure the horse from the center of its chest in a straight line across its body. This will give you the length your horse needs.

*Give the measurements to a saddler, who will work out the size you need.*

## Putting on a blanket

A horse's coat must lie flat under its blanket so it is comfortable. The fastenings must be tight enough to keep the blanket in place, but not so tight they restrict or cut into the horse.

*Modern blankets are machine washable. Keep them clean to prevent skin problems.*

**A high-cut blanket** on the neck will be less likely to slip backward than one which is cut low on the neck.

1 **Place the blanket** Fold the blanket in half from the back to the front and place it over the withers. Slide the blanket back so the horse's coat lies flat underneath, and fold down the back half.

*The blanket should not press on the horse's chest.*

# Types of blanket

There are many different types of blankets. A stable blanket keeps the horse warm and clean. It is easy to wash and can be worn daily. Summer sheets are made of light cotton to keep dust and flies off a stabled, groomed horse. Sweat sheets and coolers allow the horse's sweat to evaporate.

**Stable blankets** do not need to be waterproof. You may need to use more than one blanket on your horse as the weather gets very cold.

## BLANKETS

- A well-fitting blanket should not slip backward or rub your horse

- Each horse should have its own blankets to avoid spreading infections

- Keep spare blankets in case one gets damaged

- Clean winter blankets before storing them

**Outdoor or New Zealand rugs** must be waterproof. They are available in canvas and many modern lightweight materials.

**Summer sheets** are usually made from cotton.

**Traditional sweat sheets** are used with a blanket or summer sheet laid over the top, to trap a layer of air.

*Blanket should cover the withers at the front.*

**Cross surcingles** help prevent excess pressure on horse's spine.

*Some surcingles are elasticated.*

**2 Fasten the front straps**
Fasten the blanket leaving a hand's width between the blanket and the horse's body.

**3 Fasten the cross surcingles**
The cross surcingles fasten around the horse's girth. Adjust the straps leaving a hand's width between them and the horse.

# HEALTH AND FIRST AID

REGULAR DEWORMING, teeth rasping, and vaccinations against influenza and tetanus are vital to keep a horse healthy. Your vet can advise you about these. Learn to recognize when a horse might be ill, and how to take its temperature, and check its pulse and respiration (breathing) rate. If in doubt or worried, always call a vet.

STERILE PAD

SCISSORS

COLD TREATMENT PACK

ANTISEPTIC LIQUID

**FIRST AID KIT**
Keep a first-aid kit at the stable and take it with you when you go to shows. Your vet will advise you what to include in the kit.

**Eyes** should be fully open and bright, with no discharge.

## Checking your horse
Check your horse every day for signs of injury or illness. As you get to know your horse you will be able to tell if it is not well. A healthy horse is alert and appears happy.

*A sore back can be a sign of a badly fitting saddle.*

**Tail** should be relaxed, not clamped down.

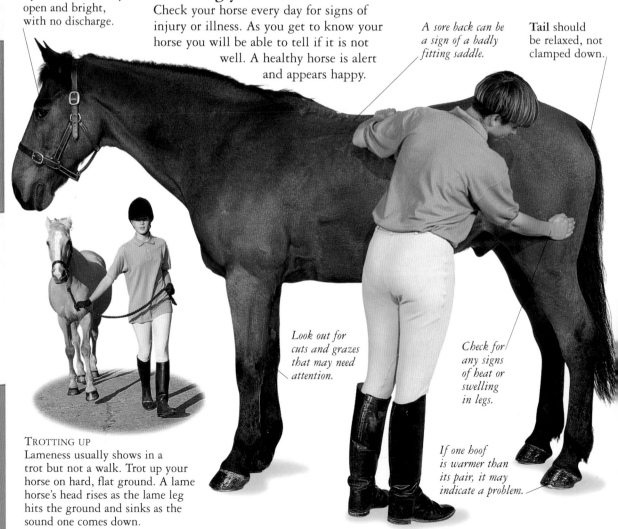

*Look out for cuts and grazes that may need attention.*

*Check for any signs of heat or swelling in legs.*

TROTTING UP
Lameness usually shows in a trot but not a walk. Trot up your horse on hard, flat ground. A lame horse's head rises as the lame leg hits the ground and sinks as the sound one comes down.

*If one hoof is warmer than its pair, it may indicate a problem.*

## Preventing illness

It is better to prevent disease than to have to treat it once it occurs. All horses should be dewormed and vaccinated regularly. They should also have their teeth checked and rasped at least once a year. Daily checks and correct management and feeding help prevent illness.

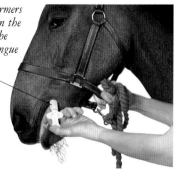

*Paste wormers are put on the back of the horse's tongue using a syringe.*

CHECKING PULSE
A normal pulse in an adult horse ranges from 35 to 45 beats per minute. The pulse will be faster in hot weather or when the horse has worked hard.

*One of the easiest places to take the pulse is where the facial artery crosses the horse's jaw bone.*

DEWORMING
Horses should be dewormed every few weeks. There are many different types of worms; ask your vet's advice on which types of wormers to use and when to give them.

## WHEN TO CALL THE VET

Always call the vet if you are worried about something, however small. Suspected colic or laminitis, or wounds spurting blood, are always emergencies. A vet should always be called if lameness is severe or prolonged, or if a wound may need stitching.

### COMMON AILMENTS

**COLIC**
Colic is another word for abdominal pain or stomach ache. Horses cannot be sick, so colic is always serious. Call your vet as soon as you suspect that something is wrong. Some cases may need surgery.

SIGNS OF COLIC

*Sweating, rolling, and kicking at the belly are all signs of colic.*

**GENERALLY SICK**
Always call your vet if you think your horse might need treatment. Describe the symptoms or injury carefully. With suspected illness, it may be useful to take the horse's temperature.

**BAD CUT**
Any cut that is longer than 1 in (2.5 cm) or gapes open may need stitching. Puncture wounds and those near joints may also need veterinary attention. Be safe, not sorry!

**LAMINITIS**
Laminitis is a painful hoof condition that is especially common in ponies. It is often linked to eating rich grass and usually affects the front hooves, so the pony tries to put more weight on its back ones. Your vet may recommend special shoes for your pony to wear.

**ARTERIAL BLEEDING**
If bright red blood spurts from a wound, your horse has probably severed an artery. Press a clean cloth firmly over the wound to limit the bleeding until the vet arrives.

**PROLONGED LAMENESS**
Always rest a lame horse. If very mild lameness lasts for more than two days, or if you are unsure, call your vet. Conditions such as tendon injuries or pulled muscles can get worse and need immediate treatment, so again, call your vet.

SITES OF LAMENESS

*Most causes of lameness occur in the hoof, such as bruises and puncture wounds.*

**SEVERE LAMENESS**
A horse that is very lame or unable to put its injured hoof on the ground is an emergency case. With suspected fractures, try to keep the horse still until the vet arrives. This prevents the injury from getting worse.

# CARE OF TACK

TACK MUST BE KEPT CLEAN and in good repair. Wash the bit and clean off dried mud every time you ride. If you don't take care of your tack it will become hard and cracked and uncomfortable for the horse to wear. At least once a week, more often if possible, dismantle the tack and clean thoroughly.

POLISHING CLOTH  WASHING CLOTH  SPONGE

LEATHER DRESSING  DRESSING BRUSHES

SADDLE SOAP  STIFF BRUSH

### TACK CLEANING KIT
For general tack cleaning you need warm water, cloths and sponges, and a stiff brush to remove dirt. Use saddle soap to keep the tack supple, and apply leather dressing about once a month, especially if the tack is new.

## Tack
Every horse should have its own tack. Make sure the tack fits properly; get expert advice if you are not sure. Saddles and bridles are made from either leather or synthetic materials. Keep tack in a dry, warm place, away from damp. Dry rain soaked leather tack away from direct heat otherwise it may turn brittle.

*To hang a bridle use a special bridle rack or make your own from a round tin.*

*Wash bits in clean water.*

*Don't use metal polish on mouthpiece.*

*Only use saddle soap on leather reins.*

## Synthetic tack
Some synthetic tack, especially bridles and girths, comes in bright, cheerful colors. Synthetic tack should be wiped with a damp cloth or washed according to the manufacturer's instructions.

*Too much soap on the saddle seat may stain clothes.*

*Wash synthetic girths as often as is necessary.*

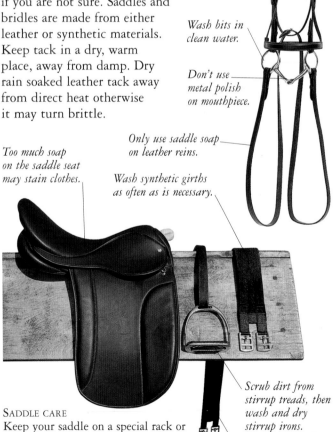

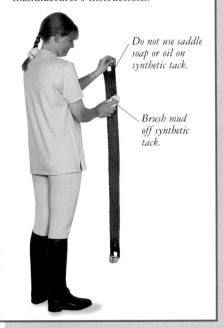

*Do not use saddle soap or oil on synthetic tack.*

*Brush mud off synthetic tack.*

### SADDLE CARE
Keep your saddle on a special rack or stand to help prevent it from getting damaged. As with all tack, the saddle should always be kept in a dry room.

*Scrub dirt from stirrup treads, then wash and dry stirrup irons.*

*Remove girth for cleaning.*

## In the tack room

Your tack room should be dry, warm, and secure. It is a good idea to install security equipment, such as alarms and a good lock. It is in the tack room that you usually clean the tack. To do this remove grease and dirt with a damp cloth, then apply saddle soap with a slightly damp sponge. Wash and rinse bits and stirrup irons, then polish with a dry cloth. Brush or wash girths and saddle pads.

**The pommel** and cantle, at the front and back of a saddle, are easily damaged.

*Bridles are easier to clean if hung from special bridle hooks.*

*Only put one saddle on each rack. Do not stack saddles.*

*Water should be warm, not hot.*

*When appling leather dressing, use a small brush.*

*Keep your saddle soap sponge damp but not wet. The soap should not foam up when you apply it.*

# TRANSPORTING A HORSE

WHEN TRANSPORTING a horse in a trailer you must aways protect it with traveling equipment, even for short journeys. The trailer should be in good condition and be large enough for a horse to travel comfortably. Horses should be tied up, but foals travel loose with their mothers. The driver should try to drive as smoothly as possible.

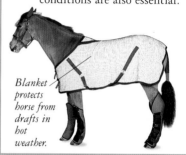

### Protecting the horse
A horse should always wear travel boots or leg wraps over padding. A tail bandage or tailguard and a blanket suitable for the weather conditions are also essential.

*Blanket protects horse from drafts in hot weather.*

## Loading up
When loading the horse into the trailer, open up the vehicle as much as possible so the horse can see where it is being asked to go. Make sure the ramp is secure, then lead the horse straight up it. Look ahead into the trailer, not back at the horse. Tie the horse up so it cannot turn around.

**The vehicle interior** should be light and inviting as horses do not like walking into dark places.

*Provide a small haynet to prevent horse becoming bored during the journey.*

**WARNING!**
Only load into an unhitched trailer if the rear prop stands are lowered.

*Ramp must be stable, not tipped up at one side.*

*Check that tire pressures are correct before every journey.*

## Unloading

The vehicle should be parked so that the horse has plenty of room to turn when it walks off the ramp. Make sure the ramp is stable, and lead the horse straight out so it does not bang against the side of the trailer.

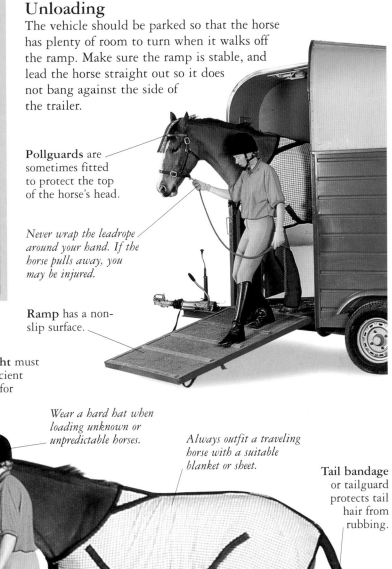

**Pollguards** are sometimes fitted to protect the top of the horse's head.

*Never wrap the leadrope around your hand. If the horse pulls away, you may be injured.*

**Ramp** has a non-slip surface.

**Roof height** must allow sufficient headroom for the horse.

*Wear a hard hat when loading unknown or unpredictable horses.*

*Always outfit a traveling horse with a suitable blanket or sheet.*

**Tail bandage** or tailguard protects tail hair from rubbing.

**Leg wraps** or bandages prevent leg injuries.

# BUYING A PONY

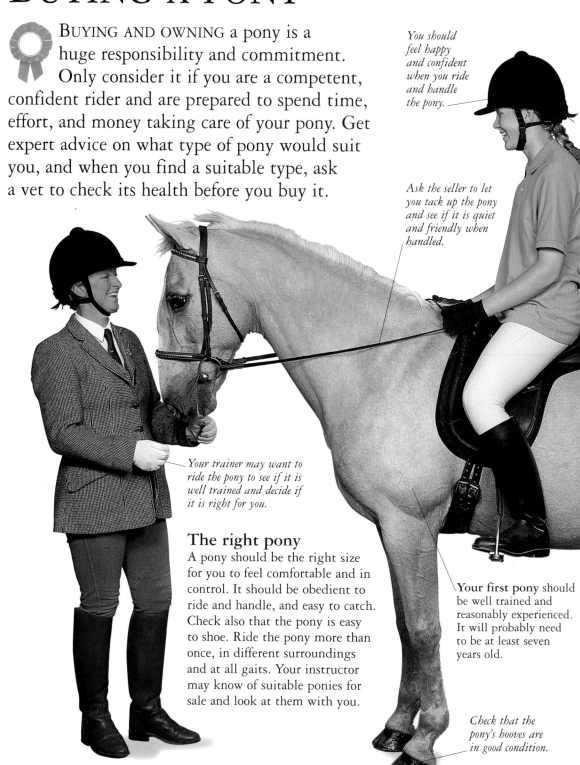

BUYING AND OWNING a pony is a huge responsibility and commitment. Only consider it if you are a competent, confident rider and are prepared to spend time, effort, and money taking care of your pony. Get expert advice on what type of pony would suit you, and when you find a suitable type, ask a vet to check its health before you buy it.

*You should feel happy and confident when you ride and handle the pony.*

*Ask the seller to let you tack up the pony and see if it is quiet and friendly when handled.*

*Your trainer may want to ride the pony to see if it is well trained and decide if it is right for you.*

## The right pony

A pony should be the right size for you to feel comfortable and in control. It should be obedient to ride and handle, and easy to catch. Check also that the pony is easy to shoe. Ride the pony more than once, in different surroundings and at all gaits. Your instructor may know of suitable ponies for sale and look at them with you.

**Your first pony** should be well trained and reasonably experienced. It will probably need to be at least seven years old.

*Check that the pony's hooves are in good condition.*

## Sharing a pony

If you can't buy a pony yet, perhaps you could share someone else's. Your trainer may know someone who would let you ride and help look after their pony in exchange for paying part of the cost of keeping it.

*Arrange cleaning shifts with your pony share partner.*

*Mucking out and grooming are all part of a sharing arrangement.*

**SPARE TIME**
Looking after a pony will take most of your spare time. It will be hard work all year round, especially in winter. You will need to get up early in the mornings.

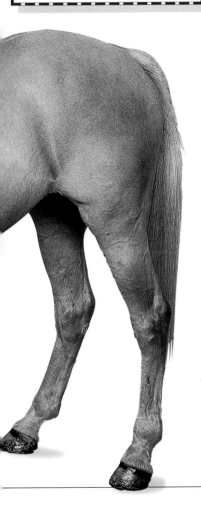

**WHERE TO KEEP YOUR PONY**
Keep your pony at a well-run stable where you can get expert help. Look for somewhere with well-built stables, and good pastures and fences. Stables which provide horse accommodation are called boarding stables.

*Find a stable where experienced people can help with any problems.*

## Vetting

Before agreeing to buy a pony, you should ask a vet to check its health and whether or not it is suitable for what you want, whether it is riding in competitions or in the countryside. This is called vetting a horse. The vet will make sure that the pony is not lame and that its eyes, heart, and lungs work properly.

*Vet uses a special instrument to check a pony's eyesight.*

# SAFETY

YOUR HORSE'S SAFETY depends on you, so check the pasture and stable area every day to make sure they are clean and safe, thus helping to prevent illness or injury. It is also important to care for your own safety by handling horses correctly and never taking risks – even quiet horses may be unpredictable if they are sick or frightened. First-aid kits for both horses and people should always be available.

## First aid for riders

Every stable should have first-aid kits for riders. Your doctor can advise you on what to include in a first-aid kit. A telephone should also be available, with emergency numbers displayed.

*First-aid kit includes bandages, ointments, and scissors.*

## Safety at the stable

The buildings and stalls must be kept in good repair, and tools and equipment should be stored safely when not in use. Dogs and young children should be supervised and not allowed to run around.

*Stay calm and concentrate on what you are doing. Never take risks.*

*Ears laid back show that the horse is unhappy.*

*Horses can kick forward and backward.*

*A horse may kick out, so always stand to one side of it.*

HORSE BEHAVIOR
A frightened horse will try to run away and one that is in pain may kick or be difficult to handle. When near the horse, always stand in a safe position. If you have to do something the horse may object to, tie up the horse. If necessary, ask for help.

# KEEPING YOUR HORSE SAFE

Daily checking of the pasture and fencing, and careful stable management will help you create a safe environment for your horse. By performing these checks you will minimize the risks to your horse of both illness and injury, for example from broken fencing. It is also important to take precautions against theft and fire.

## IN THE STABLE

### STABLE MANAGEMENT
Keep the stable clean and dust-free. Provide the horse with a deep bed, so that it doesn't injure itself on the stable floor. Disinfect the floor and walls at least twice a year. Wash buckets every day.

### SECURITY
Protect your horse from theft by using a security marking system such as freeze marking. Mark tack and equipment with your name or address. Stable your horse where someone lives on site.

### FIRE PRECAUTIONS
Keep a fire extinguisher and hose in clear view so that everyone can see where they are. Make sure electricity supplies are safe and kept away from water sources.

### KEEPING STABLE IN GOOD REPAIR
Stables should be kept in good repair so that there are no visible nails, broken wood, or other sharp objects that could injure a horse. Doors should have latches at top and bottom, so that they can be shut tight when the horse is in the stable.

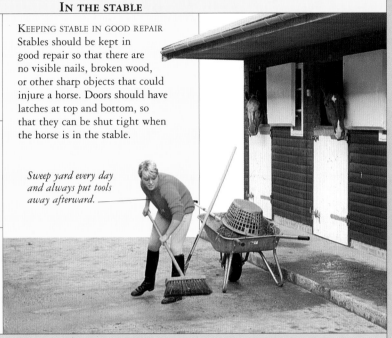

*Sweep yard every day and always put tools away afterward.*

## AT PASTURE

*Always provide clean water.*

### CHECKING WATER SUPPLY
Use a container that horses cannot knock over to provide a constant supply of clean water. These should not have any sharp edges or projections that could injure a horse. Keep container free from debris, such as fallen leaves, and if necessary, break any ice.

### FILLING IN HOLES
Use spare soil to fill in holes in the pasture made by rabbits, moles, or other animals. If a horse puts its foot down a hole it could break its leg. If your pasture has a lot of holes, get expert advice on pest control.

### KEEPING THE PASTURE CLEAN
Remove manure as often as possible, preferably every day. This helps to reduce the amount of worm eggs that live in horse manure, thus lessening health risks to the horse. Get advice on harrowing large pastures.

### REMOVING POISONOUS PLANTS
Learn to identify poisonous plants such as ragwort, yew, and deadly nightshade. Remove and burn them. Acorns are poisonous, so fence off oak trees and their surroundings.

### CHECKING FENCING
Check fencing daily for weak or broken parts. Electric fencing must be correctly installed; check that nothing is touching the electrified parts, thus causing a short circuit. If you are unsure, ask an expert how to use electric fencing.

# HORSE CARE

ROUTINE CARE, such as grooming, is the responsibility of those looking after a horse or pony – usually you. Other tasks, such as vaccinating, must be done by qualified professionals. Never forget preventative measures such as deworming, or your horse's health will suffer.

| JOB | DESCRIPTION |
|---|---|
| SIGNS OF ILL HEALTH | Always be alert for signs that a horse may be sick or injured. Danger signs include heat or swelling in the legs, restlessness and sweating, eye or nasal discharge, labored breathing, and listlessness. |
| DEWORMING | Deworming is giving a medical paste from syringes directly into a horse's mouth, or putting granules into the feed. The vet will advise you on which products to use. |
| VACCINATE | All horses should be vaccinated against tetanus and equine influenza. Brood mares may need extra vaccinations, so check with the vet. |
| SHOEING | All horses should have their hooves trimmed regularly to prevent them growing too long. Most horses need to wear shoes if they are ridden regularly. |
| RASP TEETH | Sharp teeth and hooks (curved projections on a tooth) are filed down using special dental equipment. |
| CHECK PASTURE | Check the pasture for broken or weak fencing and repair when needed. Remove and burn poisonous plants and any trash. Fill in holes made by small animals. Remove manure. |
| GROOMING | Stabled horses need to be groomed thoroughly. Pastured horses need coat oils for protection, so just brush off dried mud and groom mane and tail. |
| CLIPPING | This is the removal of all, or parts, of a horse's winter coat, using special electric or battery-operated equine clippers. |
| TACK FIT | Check that the bit, bridle, and saddle are the correct size and tack is not damaged or faulty. |

*Trotting up horse to observe its movement.*

*Feeding a pony*

**Blankets** need to be put on horses that are clipped or have thin winter coats. A sick horse will need rugs to keep it warm. Take off and replace blankets at least once a day.

PUTTING ON A BLANKET

CLEANING OUT TOOLS

**Cleaning out** every day keeps a horse's stall free from harmful gases given off by wet, dirty bedding. Store tools safely after use.

| FREQUENCY | WHO DOES IT | WHY |
|---|---|---|
| Each time you see the pony, especially first thing in the morning. | You or anyone else responsible for the horse's care. | The sooner potential problems are spotted, the more likely it is that the horse will make a quick recovery. In colic cases, speedy action can save a horse's life. |
| Every six to eight weeks on veterinary advice. | You – ask someone to show you how to administer paste. | All horses have some worms in their intestines. Deworming reduces the amount of worms in the body to a safe level. |
| A primary course is followed by annual boosters. | Vet | To protect horses against conditions that can, at times, be fatal. |
| Every four to six weeks. | A farrier. Only a registered farrier can shoe horses. | Domestic horses' hooves do not wear down fast enough, unlike those of wild horses, which are constantly on the move. |
| Once or twice a year, depending on needs of individual horse. | Vet or trained equine dentist. | Rasping teeth helps keep a horse comfortable when it is wearing a bit. It also improves a horse's ability to chew and digest food. |
| Every day | You or anyone else responsible for the horse's care. | Check the pasture to keep horse from escaping and to prevent injury or illness. Removing manure helps reduce amount of worms. |
| Every day | You or anyone else responsible for the horse's care. | Helps keep coat and skin healthy and helps you spot wounds, heat, or swelling. |
| Up to three times a year once horse's winter coat is fully grown. | Must be done by an experienced adult. | Enables horse to work without sweating too much. |
| Check for safety every time you ride. Check saddle fit every month. | Always get expert advice, especially for saddles and bits. | Badly fitting tack can cause discomfort, injury, and poor performance. |

*Cleaning the nose*

# Glossary

There are many words associated with horses. Some have been used in this book and can be found, with a description of their meaning, below.

**Blanket clip** A clip that leaves a blanket-shaped area on horse's body. Coat is also clipped from neck and belly.

**Boarding stable** Stable that provides accommodation for other people's horses and ponies.

**Body brush** Grooming brush with short bristles, used to remove oil from stabled horse's coat.

**Breastplate** This prevents saddle from slipping too far back – often used by event riders.

**Browband** Part of bridle that fits below ears and across top of horse's head; helps keep bridle in place.

**Cob** Type of riding or driving horse with powerful neck and hind-quarters, deep body, and short legs. Show cobs must be over 14.2 hh but not exceed 15.1 hh; only Welsh cobs are a breed.

**Colic** Abdominal pain, which must be treated as an emergency. Signs include kicking or biting at belly, sweating, and pawing ground.

**Cooler** Type of blanket made from absorbent fabric, which helps to dry a sweating horse.

**Cross surcingles** Blanket straps, often elasticized and made of nylon, which cross and fasten under a horse's belly to keep blankets in place.

**Curry comb** Metal or rubber grooming tool used for cleaning brushes. Rubber curry comb can be used to remove dried mud from horse's coat.

**Dandy brush** Grooming brush with stiff bristles for removing mud and loose hairs from horse's coat.

**Dewormer** Drugs in paste of granule form that should be given to horses about every six weeks to reduce number of internal worms.

**Farrier** A person who puts on horse shoes.

**Forage** Grass and hay, the most important parts of any horse's diet.

**Freeze marking** Painless form of security marking in which horse is cold-branded with unique series of letters and numbers.

**Fly fringe** Fringe attached to horse's halter, which falls across the face and helps keep flies away.

**Frog** Sensitive V-shaped fleshy area on the underside of the foot.

**Gauze** Padding used under leg bandages, in the stable, or when traveling.

**Identichipping** Form of security marking in which a tiny identichip is injected under the skin. It can can be read with a scanner.

**Laminitis** Serious hoof condition, usually linked to pony eating too much rich grass.

**Martingale** Piece of tack used to prevent horse from raising its head too high; main types are standing and running martingales.

**New Zealand rug** Waterproof blanket used to keep horse warm and dry in the field.

**Noseband** Part of bridle that fits across horse's face and fastens above or below the bit, depending on design. Main types include drop, cavesson, Flash, and Grakle.

**Poll guard** Fastens to halter and fits over the poll (top of the horse's head) to protect it when traveling.

**Pulling** Thinning and shaping horse's mane or tail by pulling out a few hairs at a time.

**Stable blanket** Blanket used to keep horse warm in the stable – it does not need to be waterproof.

**Summer sheet** Lightweight blanket, from cotton, used in hot weather to protect from insects or drafts and to keep coat clean.

**Sweat blanket** Mesh blanket used to dry off a sweating horse. It must be used with another blanket on top to trap a layer of air.

**Tack** Collective word for saddles, bridles, and other equipment used on riding horses and ponies.

**Tail bandage** Bandage put on top of horse's tail to prevent hair from being rubbed out when traveling or to encourage a pulled tail to lie flat.

**Teeth rasping** A process in which a vet or horse dentist removes sharp edges and "hooks" on horse's teeth using special files. Teeth must be rasped at least once a year.

**Throatlatch** Part of the bridle that fastens under horse's jaw to help keep bridle in place.

**Trace clip** Type of clip in which hair is removed from lower part of neck and body, following the lines of the traces of a driving harness.

**Traveling boots** Leg protectors that safeguard horse from injury when traveling in a trailer.

**Trotting up** An action in which horse is led at trot on a straight line to identify lameness or to demonstrate horse's movement.

**Vaccinations** Injections carried out by a vet, which are essential to protect horse against tetanus and equine influenza.

**Vetting** Veterinary examination done before purchase in which vet examines horse for soundness and suitability for a particular purpose.

**Weaving** Stable vice in which horse moves its head from side to side.

**Weaving grid** V-shaped grill that fits on stable door to reduce horse's ability to weave.

# INDEX

CHECKING
A PONY

# ACKNOWLEDGMENTS

**The publishers** would like to thank the following people for their help in the production of this book.

**The author**
Carolyn Henderson has lived and worked with horses for many years. She is a regular contributor to specialist magazines such as *Horse and Hound*, and has written and edited a variety of books on all aspects of keeping, riding, and training horses.

The publishers would also like to thank the following: Hilary Bird for the index and Cheryl Telfer for additional design.

CAM Equestrian Ltd, Eardisley, Hereford, for providing images of jumping poles; Lethers, Merstham, Surrey for the loan of equipment and tack. Jackki Garnham and staff, Beechwood Riding School, Woldingham, Surrey; Sandra Waylett, Gatton Park Livery, Reigate, Surrey; Ebbisham Farm Livery Stables, Walton on the Hill, Surrey, for use of their facilities.
The models Rosie Eustace, Emma de la Mothe, Kerry Meade, Alison Forrest, and Samantha Wilkinson.

Also thanks to the horses and ponies used in photography and their owners for loaning them. These are: *Cinnamon Dust* (owned by Holly Clarke); *Ginger Pick* (owned by Sandra Waylett); *Peeping Tom* (owned by Maggie Crowley); *Blondie, Dillion,* and *Garochead April* (owned by Jakki Garnham).

Every effort has been made to adhere to latest safety standards in the making of this book.

**Picture Credits**
The publishers would like to thank the following people for their kind permission to reproduce their photographs.

**key:** *b* bottom, *c* centre, *l* left, *t* top, *r* right

**Kit Houghton:** 11*t*; 17*t*; 41*cr*;
**Bob Langrish:** 25*tr*; 30*t*; 43*t*, *br*;
**Rex Features:** 26*t*.

**Additional photography**
Other photography was taken by:
**Andy Crawford:** 42*tr*; **Peter Chadwick:** 14 *bl*; **Stephen Oliver:**

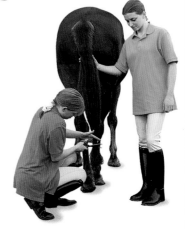

11*c*; **Ray Moller:** 17*br*; 26*tr*; **Tim Ridley:** 23*t*; 33*tr*; 45*tr*;
**Bob Langrish:** 5*tl*; 9*cl*, c; 15*tl*; 21*tl*; 22*bl*, *br*; 23*bl*, bc; 26-27; 31*cr*; 36*bl*.

With additional thanks to all the horses and ponies we photographed, and their owners. These are as follows.
**pages 8–9:** *Hippolyte,* Haras National de Pau; *Montemere O'Nora,* Nan Thurman; *Oaten Mainbrace,* Mr & Mrs Dimmock;
*Hitman,* Boyd Catrell; *Foniks,* Poul Elmerkjaer.

# Useful addresses
Here are the addresses of some societies and other organizations that you may like to contact:

**Association of Riding Establishments of Ontario**
76-7th Concession East
Milgrove, Ontario L0R 1V0
Tel: (905) 689-0683
E-mail: areont@thetackbox.com

**Canadian Veterinary Medical Association**
339 Booth Street
Ottawa, Ontario K1R 7K1
Tel: (613) 236-1162
www.cvma-acmv.org

**The Equine Research Centre**
50 McGilvray Street
Guelph, Ontario N1G 2W1
Tel: (519) 837-0061
Fax: (519) 767-1081
www.erc.on.ca

**Canadian Pony Club**
Box 4256
Station E
Ottawa, Ontario K1S 5B3
Toll-Free Tel: 1-888-286-PONY
Fax: (403) 230-PONY
www.ebtech.net/ponyclub

**Canadian Pony Society**
R.R.1
Jarvis, Ontario N0A 1J0
Tel: (905) 768-1252

**Canadian Sport Horse Association**
Box 98, 40 Elizabeth Street
Okotoks, Alberta T0L 1T0
Tel: (403) 938-0887
Fax: (403) 938-5441
www.canadian-sport-horse.org

**Canadian School of Horseshoeing**
R.R.2
Guelph, Ontario N1H 6H8
Tel: (519) 824-5484
www.horseshoes.com

**The Guild of Professional Farriers**
P.O. Box 684
Locust, North Carolina 28097
E-mail: theguild@horseshoes.com

**Mike Goodall Saddlery**
Master Saddler
P.O. Box 450
Fort St. James, BC V0J 1P0
Tel: (250) 996-7923
Fax: (250) 996-7915
www.glynx.com/biz/saddles